THE PATIENCE STRONG OMNIBUS

By the same author

TAPESTRIES OF TIME
YESTERDAYS AND TOMORROWS

THE PATIENCE STRONG OMNIBUS

A Personal Selection from Fifty Years of Verse

HUTCHINSON
London

© Patience Strong 1986

The right of Patience Strong to be
identified as the Author of this work has been asserted
by Patience Strong in accordance with the
Copyright, Designs and Patents Act, 1988

All rights reserved

First published in 1986 by Muller, Blond & White Ltd
Reprinted by Frederick Muller, an imprint of
Century Hutchinson Ltd, 20 Vauxhall Bridge Road,
London SW1V 2SA

Reprinted 1989 (twice), 1990

This edition first published in 1992 by Hutchinson
Reprinted 1992 (twice), 1993

Random Century Group Ltd
20 Vauxhall Bridge Road, London SW1V 2SA

Random Century Australia (Pty) Ltd
20 Alfred Street, Milsons Point, Sydney, NSW 2061, Australia

Random Century New Zealand Ltd
PO Box 40–086, Glenfield, Auckland 10, New Zealand

Random Century South Africa (Pty) Ltd
PO Box 337, Bergvlei, 2012, South Africa

A CIP catalogue record for this book is available from the
British Library

0 09 177330 X

Set in Palatino
Printed and bound in Great Britain by
Cox & Wyman Ltd, Reading, Berkshire

Contents

OLD MOTHER NATURE

The whole web of life is held together by unseen threads of relationships between human beings and animals, but the most marvellous relationship of all is that which binds us to Old Mother Nature.

Spring

*O*nly a God with a thinking Mind could have thought up the joys of Spring—tinting the grass with an emerald dye and teaching the birds to sing—covering hazels with powdery tassels that shimmer in every breeze—spraying the almonds with rosy pink petals and hanging the cherry trees—with bridal-white blossom, and staining the copses with patches of flowers growing wild: celandines, violets, bluebells and primroses, lovely and undefiled.

Only a God with a loving heart could have made us a world like this—where you wake up one morning and find the air as soft and as warm as a kiss—A world where like magic the daffodils come with their trumpets all glowing and bright—as if He repeated the Genesis fiat and said again, Let there be light . . . Blind evolution could not of itself have created a butterfly's wing—Only a God could have ever designed it— so praise Him, the God of the Spring.

Somehow Things Come Right

A mountain loomed before me—too steep for me to scale—and suddenly I saw It: that pathway through the vale—where cliffs of rock rose steeply to block the forward view—but somehow I was guided. Somehow I got through.

A problem like a mountain I saw confronting me: a trouble overwhelming. No hope there seemed to be—of finding a solution. But someone must have prayed—for help to me was given. The right decision made.

It seems that unseen forces are rushed to meet our need. God sends a guardian angel to strengthen and to lead—when stricken in the darkness and lost without a light. I know not how it happens, but somehow things come right.

The Rifts That Make The Glory

*I*t's not until the clouds are broken that you realize—that behind them there was an expanse of golden skies . . . It's the rifts that make the glory. When they break apart—you can see the shining edges where the sunrays start.

Always on the other side of every cloud in view—the sun is waiting glowing in a sky of heavenly blue . . . Here there is a parable for all who can discern. In the clouds there is a lesson for the heart to learn.

Every cloud of disappointment or adversity—hides the sunshine of God's presence—Him we cannot see—behind the stormy clouds that loom like mountains in the sky—but we see the Light Eternal when the clouds pass by.

Make It A Wonderful Day

Whatever the weather with sky black or blue—Whatever the problem that's troubling you—Whatever the prospect, whatever you do—make it a wonderful day . . . How is it done when the clouds draw a blind—over the brightness? It's all in the mind. Make your own glory wherever you go—seeing the sun through the rain and the snow.

When you awake in the morning from sleep—don't let your thoughts slip away and go deep—into old grooves of depression. Take charge. Your willpower assert and your vision enlarge . . . Turn them by force to the right attitude—away from the wrong and the negative mood. You are the master, so they must obey. Make it a wonderful day.

So Good A Land

*W*here else could you see in such a very tiny space—so much beauty? Tell me, is there any other place—on this overcrowded earth where you with one brief look—could see a bluebell wood, a fairy glade, a rushy brook—and a field of wheat beyond where flowery verges drift—in a haze of clover, daises, columbine and thrift?

Move the eye a fraction and your vision will extend—taking in the view that opens where the meadows end—and you see a cottage deep in clouds of applebloom—underneath a hill ablaze with gorse and yellow broom.

Where else are such pictures set within a frame so small? Only in our little England do the soft rains fall—in gentle showers that bring to life the seeds that make the green. Where else will you find so good a land, so fair a scene?

Winter's Gift

Bone bare trees against a sullen sky. Fog and frost and wet winds shrieking by. Raw dark mornings and tracks of rutted mire—leading to hayrick, stable, barn and byre.

This is the winter in the country's heart—a grey isolation in a world apart—but this, too, is winter as the long night falls: the flicker of firelight on familiar walls.

There is a healing in the winter's mood. Sated on summer's ripened plenitude—I walk in the quiet fields—and gratefully feed on the gleanings of austerity.

Always New

I thought I knew all about roses—but every time they appear—I see as a bright bud uncloses—a beauty unnoticed last year . . . They never repeat a performance—No season is ever the same . . . I thought I had seen all the colours, the crimson, the gold and the flame—but here is a rose peeping in at the door. I swear that I never saw this one before.

I thought I knew all about thrushes—but I must admit I was wrong—At dusk or when morning sky flushes—they come with a new kind of song . . . The notes they have practised since Eden—I know them by heart theme by theme—and yet when they sing in my garden—I listen as if in a dream—They sing the old songs with the same measured range—yet something about it is wondrous and strange . . . Bored we become with what science supplies—but Nature is always an endless surprise.

Life Flashes By

Midsummer Day has come and gone. Slowly the sun now loses height. Summer's rich splendour lingers on. Roses still cluster, but day and night—the glory is waning. The peak is passed. Time makes its reckoning all too fast.

Life flashes by as we older grow. Each passing year rushes swifter by. Where do the runaway seasons go? Vainly we wonder and question why—but we can't bid the beautiful moments stay—or call back one hour of a a lovely day.

Gather your memories secretly—so you can dream when you are old—living on Summer's legacy. Even though life turns grey and cold— you will never feel lonely, lost or sad—recalling the happy times you had.

Spring Was Yesterday

*I*t was only yesterday that I looked out to see—blackbirds nesting in the hedge and blossom on the tree—daffodils and hyacinths—and now the creepers glow—rose and crimson on the wall. Where did the Summer go?

In a flash it came and went. I tried to hold it back—by counting every moment, but it passed and in its track—Autumn weaves a leafy carpet, russet, flame and red—where the golden goblets of the crocuses were spread.

Why does time increase its pace? It should be otherwise. Every year should be longer but each one swifter flies . . . Summers used to linger, now they hurry on their way. Looking back it seems to me that Spring was yesterday.

Rose In The Rain

Rose at the window pressed close to the pane—lifting your face to the tears of the rain—over the hill, reaching up from the spray—Joy you have brought to an invalid's day.

Seen through the sheen of the silvery shower, keeping me company hour after hour—bright in the lightning that splinters the sky—poised on your stem with the wind blowing by.

Rose at the window—I've watched from my bed—and lovely you looked with the storm overhead—What is the magic? The secret explain—How to hold on till the sun comes again.

Younger You Would Like To Grow

Younger you would like to grow, but even if you could—Would you really wish to go right back to babyhood? Wouldn't it be awful if you had to face the years—dwindling back to childhood with its tantrums and its tears.

Growing old we all regret, but it is better far—than getting younger day by day, things being what they are . . . Wisely did the good Lord plan that we like swelling grain—should grow towards maturity and growing older gain—the wisdom and the understanding that the years can bring—if we go on looking forward, learning, ripening.

Every day add something to the treasury of Time—so that when you get beyond the zenith of your prime—you don't go back, but onward and you welcome every stage—richer, stronger, wiser for the garnerings of age.

A Change of Mood

*T*here's a wintry touch in the air today, a fleck of frost on the holly spray—and more than a whispered hint of death in the smell that comes on the wind's rough breath: the smell of leaves that decaying lie—under the grey and grieving sky.

But a change of season need only be—a change of rhythm, a change of key—a different mood and another phrase—in the symphony of the passing days . . . Summer and Autumntide, Winter, Spring. Each has it's own good gift to bring . . . Enjoy then the year with it's changing themes—thankful because there are no extremes.

Travel the world and you'll never find—a climate where Nature is half so kind . . . Gently we pass from the Autumn's glow—to the Winters that bring but a little snow: a few brief weeks when the birds are dumb—when the long nights drag and the sharp frosts come—but even when April seems far away—God often sends us a beautiful day.

Bubbles In The Sky

*H*ow lovely are the clouds of March—under heaven's spreading arch! Foamy chariots riding by—across the highways of the sky . . . Upward we look surprised to see—so huge a mass move suddenly—like a thousand flags unfurled—above the mountains of the world.

And when a driving wind prevails—they resemble billowing sails—dipping across the waves of space—as if competing in a race . . . Feather-light the big clouds break—Bursting like bubbles they froth and flake—floating off into the blue—beyond the measure of our view.

The Holidays

*T*rain the children not to waste the precious holiday hours—Teach them how to think and look at berries, leaves and flowers—Educate the little ones to study Nature's ways—Open a new and wonderful world for them in holidays.

Freed from the schoolroom let them wander, wondering at it all—Let them see the glorious splendour of a waterfall—Draw their active minds away from mere mechanical toys—discovering the magic of strange things and deeper joys.

Of richly-painted butterflies and graceful birds in flight—of sun and shadow breaking through the curtain of the light—Woods where great trees lean above a softly singing brook—Feed them with the knowledge to be found in Nature's book.

The Bend By The Signpost

We've turned the bend by the signpost that bears the word to Spring—We've come a few steps nearer to the moment that will bring—the hallelujah choruses to garden, wood and lane—telling us that life is stirring in the soil again.

We've turned our backs on Winter though still the winds blow cold—we see beneath the budding tree a flash of fairy gold. Daffodils and crocuses are massing out of sight—preparing for the festival of colour, life and light. This is the month of miracles, the season of rebirth—when beauty breaks the seals and springs triumphant from the earth.

THE MAGIC OF MEMORIES

Human beings are inventive, some even clever, but no-one has ever been clever enough to explain the workings of memory. Nor has anyone been able to tell you what a memory is, where it comes from and where it goes when it has passed through the mind. Memories are our invisible companions.

Make Me A Memory

Make me a memory—something to treasure—after the glow and the glamour have gone . . . like some old melody—bringing back pleasure, strangely and tenderly lingering on.

Say something wonderful—words I'll remember—if Time in passing should tear us apart . . . Life takes its course. Love must burn to its ember. Say just one thing I can hold in my heart.

Give me a day of delight and perfection—with never a shadow, or pang of regret—a day to recall with a loving affection—to cherish for ever and never forget.

Only Another Milestone

*D*o not count the passing birthdays with a tearful sigh—Let them come and let them go as Time goes flying by—Never waste a moment on the things that you regret—If you've sought forgiveness—say Amen—and then forget.

Thank God that another year now lies ahead of you—for living and for loving—Take the optimistic view—Every day with grateful heart expect a miracle—looking out for something that is good and beautiful.

Travel hopefully along. Don't say the best has gone—Birthdays are the milestones but the road goes winding on.

Beautiful Moments

I opened wide the window to the morning of the day—and from the wintry branches of the trees across the way—I heard the robins and the thrushes fluting joyously—and it seemed that they were singing specially for me.

I stood and listened. Every note was like a silver bell—and deep inside my heart I knew: I knew that all was well. A word of hope had reached me through the birds ... I can't explain—But that lovely message had not come to me in vain. A thrill of new expectant life along my nerves had run—as, looking up, I felt the warm sweet kisses of the sun.

One Perfect Day

Did you ever live one perfect day—When everything you did or said or thought—was in the spirit of the One who brought—the light of life to guide us on our way? Did you ever feel when night brought rest—and your heavy lids began to close—that in every matter that arose— you had practised what you had professed?

No. You never did, for are not we—fallible and human? None is good. We know so much, yet have not understood—the simple truth Christ preached in Galilee . . . We fail, as all must fail unless they pray—for strength of will to keep the soul alive. Tomorrow, while there's time, resolve to strive—To conquer self—and live one perfect day.

The Harbour Of Contentment

Off to my treasure isle of dreams I sailed on the morning tide—with only my hopes for compasses and only my star to guide . . . Seeking for happiness I called at many a far strange port—then on I sailed unsatisfied, for I knew not what I sought.

Over the oceans of the years I travelled but never found—the lost horizon; so sick at heart I turned my ship around—towards the place I had started from. To that haven of rest I went—home on the flow of the evening tide to the harbour of content—There to discover what I had wandered round the world to find. It was there all the time awaiting me: contentment and peace of mind.

The Key Word

Do you think that happiness resides in just what you possess? Seek that happiness within—and every morning will begin—with thoughts of joy and gratitude—Cultivate the attitude—that life is sweet and life is good—if God's great laws are understood.

Do not say you cannot see—the glimpses of divinity—behind the drab and commonplace—you feel the everlasting grace—but only with your inner sight—can you perceive this hidden light: this aura, making dull things shine—with splendour from a source benign

In the crowds that throng the street—a radiant face you seldom meet—so marked they are with lines of care. A sunny countenance is rare . . . The world with all its sham and show—can't tell you what you long to know: the key word that will heal and bless . . . The secret of true happiness.

Confession

*L*ord, I cannot see the way. So hour by hour and day by day—let me place my hand in Thine—lest I miss some vital sign—a turning to the left or right. Lord walk with me and be my sight.

Lord, I often fail to hear—Thy guiding voice although so near—for quiet is the tender word—the loving message scarcely heard—above the strident clamourings of urgent claims and wordly things.

Lord, this life is hard to live. My many weaknesses forgive—and in Thy mercy see my need. Without Thee I am lost indeed.

Power Of Happiness

When the mind is happy the heart is happy too. Picking up the message, the body takes its cue—and the feet, responding, walk with lighter tread—as thoughts like merry dancers go whirling round your head.

Brightness, like the sunshine, sparkles in your eyes. Somehow you feel better as your spirits rise . . . Hope and health together blend in harmony—Nervous tensions slacken, calmly, quietly.

Cheerfulness works wonders. Gaiety can be—potent as a tonic. Nature's remedy—for the ills and ailments that weaken and depress. Simple but effective; the power of happiness.

Somebody's Tomorrow

*I*s anyone the happier for meeting you today? Has anyone been prayed for just because he came your way? Has anyone been helped because you stopped to lend a hand—spared a little time to listen, tried to understand?

Has anyone been made to feel that God was somewhere near? Has someone somewhere been relieved of worry and of fear? . . . Has someone rediscovered faith in what is good and true— seen another side to life, another point of view?

If the answer's Yes, then you have earned your night's repose. If No, your day was wasted, spent in vain—and at its close—there can be no satisfaction; not unless you say—that somebody's tomorrow will be better than today.

Beyond The Easter Mystery

*A*t the time of daffodils—when Spring across the windy hills—comes a-dancing wild and gay—there comes this dark and solemn day, the day when God was crucified—and as a common felon died—to rise again mysteriously—the risen living Lord to be.

O miracle most marvellous that God could come and suffer thus! To reappear and reassure his friends, that they too could endure—what lay ahead; for He could see beyond the Easter mystery—when He, the Christ would come again—in glory and with power to reign.

The Uncompleted Tapestry

*A*fter a bereavement when the last word has been spoken—the tapestry is laid aside. The thread of life is broken—the growing pattern that evolved out of the worst and best—can never be completed now. Unfinished it must rest . . . The hand that held the needle can no longer draw the strand—but somewhere on the other side a new design is planned.

And you, now left alone, must take the skein of mingled hues, the crimsons and the violets, the scarlets and the blues—and start to work upon the uncompleted tapestry—Not the same, but different, and lovely it could be—with glowing tints of memory to give a bright relief—like threads of fire embroidered on the canvas of your grief.

The Quiet Ways

Walk slowly when you walk in lanes for there is much to see—the russet bracken on the banks, the structure of a tree—when autumn winds have stripped it naked, bare against the sky. You'll never know what you have missed, if rushed, you hurry by.

Tread softly when you enter churches. This is holy ground. A mind attuned to quietness can catch the muffled sound—of all the prayers and all the praises that have risen here. Voices echo in the silence for the listening ear.

Go gently as you go along the noisy ways of life. Move graciously amongst the crowds, the turmoil and the strife . . . Speak lovingly to children, to the stranger and the friend. Speak kindly. Never with your tongue your fellow man offend.

Old is Beautiful

A church or a cathedral, brick and stone—stained by Time in every mellow tone—of gold, moss-green and grey. The hallowed walls—seem to be alive when sunlight falls—on altar, lectern, windowpane and pew—with a sense of peace surrounding you . . . Old is beautiful.

A face—where there is written line by line—the manuscript of life; the open sign—displaying what the changing years have wrought—Eyes where joy lights up each passing thought. Hands grown frail with work done willingly—in the service of Love's ministry . . . Old is beautiful.

When I Said Goodbye To You

I said goodbye to the Summer when I said goodbye to you—I said goodbye to the roses, to the sea and the downland view—It was a wonderful Summer, but all the time I knew—It could not last forever. No dream like that comes true.

And so we floated together, as on a tide of dreams—A brief but strange encounter, incredible it seems—viewed from across the river of everyday concerns—A little candle of happiness was lighted and still burns—in the hidden cavern of that secret place—where I keep the memories that time can never efface.

It's All In The Logbook

It's all in the logbook: the ports of call, the daily incidents—the warnings, the weather, the calms, the storms, the hour-to-hour events . . . The maritime journal must be completed be it dark or light—the readings of compasses, charts and stars—all there in black and white.

And every soul is a kind of ship as the sea of life it sails—every detail of what occurs in sunshine or in gales—is all in the logbook; good deeds and bad. The truth you cannot hide—when the Pilot takes you into harbour on the evening tide.

The Way I Used To Take

*T*his is the way I used to take —Up through the woods that fringed the lake—Over the hill and into the lane—Down to the village then home again . . . Past the old church with its Saxon well, its Norman font and its English bell—Under the bridge where the kingfishers flew—at the river's edge where the cowslips grew.

This is the way I used to take—Never foreseeing that man would make—a hell of my heaven: an ugly place—devoid of beauty and of grace . . . Lacking in character, naught left to feed—the heart in its spiritual need. House by house identical. Every one with its aerial. Is this the way I used to take—or am I dreaming wide awake?

Three Eyes

*I*nsight, foresight, hindsight. We have within the mind—the power of looking inwardly, and forward and behind—wonderfully are we made. This is a mystery—how in separate directions we can look . . . and see.

No-how can we understand the workings of the brain—how thoughts can switch from off the track, can go and come again—Delving down into ourselves then flashing suddenly—forward to the future and then back via memory.

TAKE A LITTLE TIME

Take a little time for seeing—grass and blooms with dew impearled—Take a little time for being—Quiet in your own small world . . . Take a little time for sowing— flowers amongst life's many weeds— Someday you will see them glowing— growing from the hidden seeds.

Take a little time to ponder—what is in your secret heart—Take a little time to wander—in the silence set apart . . . Take a little time for living—busy though your day may be—Take a little time for giving— happiness to somebody.

The House of Remembering

*H*ow could I not remember you—when at every turn—you move amongst the shadows where the lamps of memory burn? Something of you lingers still around the home we made—for happiness paints its pictures in tints that never fade.

Sometimes I catch an echoing, so soft that I scarcely hear. I open a door and seem to feel you intimately near—No sadness marks your coming and going. In every room you leave—a joy beyond the power of telling. Why then should I grieve?

Friends say this house is haunted—why not look for somewhere new—but how could I bear to go? Here I belong because of you . . . Here then I shall stay as one by one the years slip on—for in some other place perhaps I'd find that you had gone.

The Greatest Gift

Give your child a good foundation in the things that matter—then when come the shocks and disappointments they won't shatter—their faith in life; if kicked around on solid ground they'll fall—knowing there's a God above who is the judge of all.

You can give your child no greater treasure than The Book—in which the laws of life are written. Make them learn and look—and find the secret blessing that mere money cannot buy. With this they'll have the power to fight, all evil to defy.

Do not satisfy their cry for every trivial thing—give them words of wisdom and your precious gift will bring—something that will give a beauty to the fresh young face—the refinement of the touch of spiritual grace: a light to banish doubts and fears—and lead them safely through the years.

Where Day Meets Night

I walk in my garden in the evening hours—for this is the moment to commune with flowers. The dusk drops its curtain and it seems to me— they too are conscious of a mystery—For when they are smiling in the sun's full glare—of me and my presence they are unaware—sharing their secrets with the singing birds—lost in an ecstasy that knows no words.

But when I seek them and the hour is late— they meet my mood and we are intimate . . . I touch them lovingly though veiled from sight— in that strange borderland where day meets night.

Let Love Speak

Let the word of peace be spoken—when relationships are broken. Let Love speak and heal the smart—of wounds inflicted on the heart.

Let Love's language, sweet and tender—its own gentle service render—saying what is kind and wise—with the lips or with the eyes.

Let no grievance leave an ember—that perhaps you may remember—and regret in later years—with your penitential tears.

Try forgiving. Try confessing. Let Love speak the final blessing—casting every doubt away—before the closing of the day.

What Might Have Been

*T*hink of me a little as the busy days go by. Never quite forget what might have been . . . In between the crowded hours make room for memories—evoking from the past some lovely scene—a recollection from the void—of the thing we have destroyed.

For everyone there's somebody, but sometimes things go wrong—Confusion follows, and the wires get crossed . . . Foolishly mistakes are made—discordant notes creep in—and one day you discover love is lost.

My Memories

Lord, what do you ask of me, a big or little thing? Whatever it might be, I will obey . . . Take the treasure of my heart though close to it I cling—but never take my memories away . . . because they are the unseen threads that hold me to the past—without them I should lose identity . . . Deep into a grey and timeless world I should be cast—and looking back, no milestones I should see.

So be it Lord, take what you will of what I now possess. Whatever be demanded I will pay: sight or hearing, health and strength, life's greatest happiness—but never take my memories away.

Feeling Hurt

*H*owever hurt you're feeling—hide the secret scar—Time will bring its healing. See things as they are.

Try to be forgiving—loving more, not less. Life is meant for living and for happiness . . . Maybe someone somewhere is feeling sorry too—longing for the whisper of a word from you.

Time To Go

*T*he last rose lingers on into December—clinging to the skirts of old November—Like a ballerina ageing fast—who wants to go on dancing to the last.

Sad, but proud, unwilling to surrender—dreaming of the heyday of her splendour . . . Tears of rain from off her petals flow—as the cold wind whispers, "Time to go".

Lose Yourself In Other People's Troubles

Lose yourself in other people's troubles—by lending them a sympathetic ear—for troubles lost perhaps will be forgotten—and in the end will even disappear.

Lose yourself in what is all around you. The whole wide world outside your door is there— with neighbours, colleagues, relatives and strangers—who too have crosses difficult to bear.

So if you're feeling lonely or despondent—just treading up and down the same old ways—go take a look at other people's problems—and lose yourself in someone else's maze.

The Puzzle

A sparkle of light on the floor I could see—A bead or the stone from a brooch it could be—I stooped to retrieve it, but nothing was there. My fingers outreaching clutched only the air . . .

It was a sunbeam entrapped in a ray—that somehow from millions of miles far away—had come from the big burning ball of the sun—where its long journey to earth had begun.

Foolish to snatch at this flicker of light—Trying to capture a jewel in flight. How came the sunbeam to fall on my mat? Useless to ask such a question as that. Why pose a puzzle none can expound—tapping at doors where no answer is found?

Learning To Count

When folks complain you sometimes wonder if they ever had—the sort of education that would teach them how to add . . . You do not have to get degrees life's problems to surmount—All you have to do is stir your memory and count . . . your blessings day by day . . . If you can't see them you must be—mentally blind or deaf, for all around your eyes should see—evidence of things you took for granted through the years—So instead of boring people with your trials and tears—Reach for pad and pencil and each day write out a list—of mercies granted, blessings sent—and let not one be missed.

Teaching The Children

*T*here's time to eat, but seldom time to think—
Time to wash the dishes in the sink—but seldom
time to spare or time to give—in teaching the little
ones how best to live—How to speak and how to
train the mind—the pearls of truth and wisdom
there to find.

Try not to miss the opportunity—to lift the veil
upon the mystery—of life itself and what it's all
about—Teach them the Way, dispelling every
doubt—Protect them and direct them to the
Man—who died to give the world a master plan.

THE HAPPY PEOPLE

Who are the happy people? The people who are free—from self and its dictation, the people who can be—quiet and unoffended when hurt or brushed aside—not concerned with saving their faces or their pride . . . These are the happy people. They never have to fight—to express a grievance or maintain a right.

The unassuming people of little wordly worth. What did the Master promise? He promised them the earth! The gentle-hearted people who don't ask much of life—are rich in all that matters. Content, avoiding strife . . . Never provoking trouble or stirring enmity. These are the happy people for they are truly free.

Something Happens When You Smile

When you come to think of it a smile's a funny thing. Give it and you get it back, and often it will bring—happiness to somebody you never even knew: neighbours, fellow-travellers or strangers in the queue.

Lift the corners of your lips and in the glass you'll see—a transformation and a change of personality . . . Eyes can smile as well as lips. They catch your mood and glow—even though your heart be breaking and your spirits low.

Practise at the mirror when a moment you can spare. Try. You'll be surprised to see the face reflected there . . . Somehow you seem brighter and you feel that life's worthwhile. Isn't it amazing? Something happens when you smile.

A Year Is Born

We wish each other happiness as every new year chimes. And we want it for ourselves, good days and happy times—but do we make too much of it and is there too much stress—laid on the importance of this thing called happiness?

A happy and a bright new year; the customary phrase! Happiness is sweet . . . but in these grim and troubled days—May it be a useful year, a year of work well done; a busy year of goals attained and moral battles won.

It's a strange and holy moment when from belfry towers—the clocks strike out the solemn message of the midnight hours. A year is born . . . O pray for wisdom as it comes to birth—to do your share and build God's kingdom here upon the earth.

Harmony

*L*et us work for Harmony in every walk of life; harmony instead of discord, jealousy and strife; if we live in harmony, no jarring note destroys peace of mind—relationships, and all our precious joys.

Harmony of voices. Let no ugly sound be heard—bickering or bitterness, the shrill and angry word; may the voices in the house be soothing and refined; quiet and happy, saying only what is good and kind.

Harmony throughout the world. Oh, may we live to see—Christ's own Kingdom. Not a dream, but a Reality. Every nation in the world united, and yet free—working out their destinies in perfect harmony.

Between The Acts

*T*here are intervals in life. The show can't run non-stop. In between the acts there comes a pause. The curtains drop. Circumstances take a hand and something unforeseen—comes along and breaks the pattern of the old routine. Illnesses, upheavals or a cruel turn of fate—call a halt and there is nothing you can do but wait.

While you're waiting learn the grace of faith and fortitude—as your life is being changed and problems are reviewed—Intervals there have to be; accept them. Face the facts. Wisely use the quiet times that come between the acts.

Coming Or Going

*D*o not say you're going through a time of suffering. Say you're coming through it. That's a very different thing. Coming through your trouble to the brightness round the bend. Coming through the tunnel to the sunshine at the end.

Coming through with banners flying, stronger every day. Coming through, not going through—with Hope to lead the way . . . Coming through your difficulties. Coming through your test—coming through the worst and yet believing in the best . . . No matter what life does to you—Always say you're coming through.

What Shall I Give?

*W*hat shall I give? You ask each year as Christmas days draw nigh. What can I do for those I love—what present can I buy? What shall I give my feelings to express and to convey—for the festival of love we keep on Christmas Day?

What shall I give? said God, unto my children there below—struggling in the dark. What gift of joy can I bestow? . . . I will go myself, He said, as one of them to be. I will visit my creation. They My face shall see.

This will I do to prove my love and teach them how to live. More I cannot do for them and more I cannot give. I Myself will be the gift within a human frame. I will give them Christmas to remind them that I came.

Your Blessings

*T*hough you may be passing through a dark and anxious time, smile and keep your courage, for surrender is a crime. Gratitude works magic, like the waving of a wand. Lift your eyes above the shadows to the world beyond.

With a glad and grateful heart, you'll take a different view. Think of all the benefits that fate has showered on you. Do not dwell upon misfortunes and the tears you've shed; count your blessings, drop your cares, and count your joys instead.

So when in the morning you awake to greet the day, do this little sum before you go upon your way. Add up all your blessings, past and present, great and small; you will find that Life is not so empty, after all.

You'd Be Surprised

You're never as ill as you think you are so do not be dismayed—if your mirror tells you you are looking old and frayed. It's only a passing phase. You'll soon be feeling fit and fine. Tomorrow or the next day you will sparkle. Eyes will shine . . . It's wonderful how a hopeful thought can change your point of view—so that courage, health and strength come flowing back to you.

You're never as wronged as you think you are when something you resent—and never as hurt as you say when putting up an argument . . . You'd be surprised how rapidly a grievance fades away—if you can think of something else and drop it for today.

How Did It Happen?

*V*iolets by the woodland way. Promise of blossom on the spray. Wonderful glow of daffodils—underneath the windowsills—and by the verges of the lane—primroses beaded with the rain.

Glorious splash of crocus gold—as in the sun the cups unfold. Thrusting of tips where frosts still cling. Wonder of hyacinths opening. Fragrance of daphne on the breeze. Beautiful pink of almond trees. Just as if somebody overnight—had cast a spell and lit a light—by some act of wizardry. How did it happen? You tell me.

Be Your Own Best Friend

*B*e your own best friend. A friend—and not an enemy—so that if you're left alone you're in good company—Learn to love the silences that steal in here and there—as you sit and think your thoughts before an empty chair.

Know yourself and teach yourself contentedly to live—independent of the world and what it has to give . . . Train your mind to gather gold from every passing day—so that you will never have to wish the hours away.

Come to terms and to yourself a good companion be—one to be relied upon when life is out of key . . . Loneliness you'll never know and peace you will possess—if you have within yourself the root of happiness.

Not The Answer

*P*arting is not the answer . . . That way lies defeat—disaster and disruption, failure and retreat—The way together forward is the way that we must take—Resolved to face the future, side by side, without a break . . . Making something good of life and something that will last—To our wedding vows remaining true and holding fast—Not parting, but starting all over again, beginning now today—Parting is not the answer. Let us try the other way.

THE TONE
OF A HOME

One can have an intimate relationship with a home whether it be a cottage or a mansion, a flat in a busy town or a house in a suburb. A home consists of four walls. First it is formed by the impersonal hands of the builder, next it becomes the property of the people who live, sleep, eat and think in it and it is what is thought, said and done within these walls that determines the atmosphere of a home. Take care. Restrain tempers and tongues. Harbour no grievances. Let the music of kind words be the daily theme around which the tone of the home is built up and sustained.

Tongues

*S*peak with quiet reverence of spiritual things. Guard the doors of speech against the ugly word that brings—evil in its train. Take not the Lord's dear name in vain. Honour what is good and holy. Shun what is profane.

Tongues can bless and tongues can curse. Much power do tongues possess—making trouble, causing strife or bringing happiness . . . Language can be blasphemous, crude, vile and horrible—or it can be pacifying, pure and beautiful . . . Watch your tongue and let no child hear words of violence—and of Him who heareth all—speak well. Give no offence.

Happy Families

Make your home the centre of a happy family—bringing all your friends into the cosy company—where an open door is kept for all to share the fun—Dad and mother always there to care for everyone.

Grandpa, grandma, parents, children. Each has much to give—age and youth together working out the way to live—with mutual respect and lots of laughter to be heard. In such a home you seldom hear a cross or unkind word—Even if you're not all living at the same address—keep in touch inside the circle of the happiness—kindled in the gaiety—of a happy family.

Someone Built A Cottage

*S*omeone built a cottage three hundred years ago—to stand against the weather, the wind, the rain, the snow. He set it stout and sturdy upon a Sussex hill. His work was good to look at and it is lovely still . . . Upon a frame of timber the russet tiles were laid. That roof is still a fine one for it was truly made. The oak of posts and lintels hold every brick secure. Behind their screen of roses the weathered walls endure.

The beams that span the ceiling, so cosy, snug and low—reflect the shine and shadow from sun and firelight glow. The hearth that warmed his children on cold and wintry days—still gives content and comfort within its cheery blaze . . . Someone built a cottage. His name I do not know—but when he made that cottage three hundred years ago—He would have been astonished to know that it would be—a well-loved home for someone in the twentieth century.

Cheerfulness

Cheerfulness is like a lamp that radiates a light—scattering depressing thoughts and putting fears to flight—generating happiness wherever felt or heard—with an optimistic viewpoint or a cheery word.

Cheerfulness can animate the spirit of a crowd. Something happens as when sun comes breaking through a cloud . . . Some there are who have this power to be a medium—that the joy of life flows through whenever troubles come—changing situations when the atmosphere is tense—knowing how to strike the note of hope and confidence.

Grace At Table

*E*very meal is a sacrament. All bread is holy bread—because it comes from God by whom the hungry world is fed—but we, defiant of His laws, upset the balanced plan—destroying what the Lord created for the needs of man.

With fruit and wine, with corn and fish and with the flesh of beast—He prepares before our eyes a rich and goodly feast . . . When you eat remember this. Give thanks and grateful be—to Him who conjures banquets out of river, soil and sea.

Love Is . . .

Love is more than passing pleasures. Love is happiness—found in home and homely treasures that the years will bless . . . Love is caring—Love is bearing—one another's crosses. Love is sharing everything, the profits and the losses.

Love is more than bells and laughter on a wedding day. Love is facing what comes after—sunny skies or grey . . . Love is giving. Love is living just for one another—working out the daily problems of your lives—Together.

This Thing Will Pass

The wind is beating at the pane—in frantic gusts of sleeting rain—Like lashes of a whip it falls on the windows and the walls, thrashing through the tortured trees—at the house, while I at ease—sit in comfort safe and warm—from the fury of the storm.

The demon wind must spend its force—have its hour and take its course . . . Remember this when trials increase. Rest in faith and be at peace. Through the turmoil and the din—Hear that still small voice within—speak above the crashing brass—saying, "Trust. This thing will pass."

Take What Comes

Don't expect perfection for you'll never find it here. This is earth, not heaven, so with charity and cheer—take what comes, the good, the bad, and don't start whimpering—when you're disappointed with a person or a thing.

Do not worship idols and complain when you have found—feet of clay beneath the robes in which you've wrapped them round . . . Everyone is human. Do not be too critical—when someone fails. Remember that you, too, are fallible.

Keep your ideals in your heart and set your standard high—but don't lose faith when things go wrong. Just let the storm blow by . . . Do not ask too much of life or reach beyond your range. Accept and learn to live content with what you cannot change.

Silently

*S*ilently the seed swells in the earth—and the unborn child awaits its birth . . . Silently the snow falls, feather-light. Silently the stars dance through the night . . . Silently as in a lovely dream—glides the swan upon the moving stream. Silently roots spread and buds unclose. Silently dawn comes and sunset glows.

Silently the mystic meditates. Silently he watches and he waits. Silently the grail of truth is sought—in the quiet sanctuary of thought . . . Man creates the world's cacophony—by speech and motion. God works silently.

Does It Matter?

When all is said and done—Does it matter—if you're in the third or seventh place? If neighbours have some gadgets that you covet—or colleagues streak ahead in life's made race? No, if you have friends who really love you—and strength to bear the cross upon your back—So long as you can rest with conscience easy—at peace with God and man—What can you lack?

When all is said and done—Does it matter—the thing you won't forget and won't forgive . . . ? A grievance nursed can grow beyond controlling. Stop worrying. Step out of it and live.

Make Yourself At Home

Make yourself at home if you are there—
Enjoy the comfort of your garden chair. Relaxing
in the place you love the best—Forget the jobs
and give yourself a rest.

Could you face the effort and the strain—of
packing all those cases once again?—Rushing off
to Paris, Nice or Rome?—Treat yourself and
make yourself at home.

THE COMPANIONSHIP OF TREES

The place occupied in our lives by the company of trees is closely knit into our relationships with Mother Nature. Most of us at some time have known what it was to develop a love-tie with a particular tree. It was the hawthorn you passed every morning as you made your way through the local park. It was the lilac tree in your own back garden which every Spring used to tap on your shoulder with a spray of purple blossom, as if drawing attention to itself in this its "finest hour", or there was that old oak from which you drew new strength when the wind was wild and the winter bleak. These were more than companions, they had become friends, always there to hold out their own gift to meet your special need.

The Space Between

A garden cannot look its best where trees stand thick in gloom—clustered like a crowd of gossips in a dark old room ... Trees must breathe and look alive if they are to be seen—with shapely limbs upreaching from a foam of leafy green.

Grateful must they feel when someone comes with axe or blade—to cut the strangling growth; with one swift stroke a space is made—to let the sky weave soft blue ribbons round their nakedness—and the sun with golden touches comes to heal and bless.

We, too, in our crowded minds should dare at times to make—a space where God can enter in, the stranglehold to break—of clawing thoughts that tend to choke, to threaten and destroy—the best in life: things that make for light and peace and joy.

In Between The Stones

In between the stones of life there fall the wind-blown seeds—of friendship, love and loyalty, kind words and kindly deeds . . . Often they may hide for years and never form a flower—Then opportunity in passing brings the destined hour.

You never knew you'd meet someday the one you'd call a friend—to whom your heart would open and on whom you could depend—There it lay amongst the sticks, the pebbles and the cones—the seed that flowered beside life's pathway in between the stones.

First Beginnings

Lovely are the first beginnings of the autumntide—whether you wander afoot in woods or through the forests ride—as birch and bracken turn to gold and Nature holds its breath—between the days of maturity and its seeming hour of death.

Look your last on the year now dying. Look and let it go. Spring will bring its resurrection. Believe; it will be so . . . Every tree will bud, and sap will flow in every vein. Though we, like time, must go when called; the tree will live again.

The Garden Of Stillness

*H*ere is a garden of stillness where no winds run to stir—the statuesque solemnity of cypress, yew or fir—The upward sloping edges, thick with beech and birch—preserve within this sanctuary the silence of a church.

Here in this garden of quiet the mind is unaware—of the track that meets the road—a mile or less out there—As if the trees had here ordained that restlessness must cease—so that all who come may find the benison of peace.

What's The Time?

We are all so busy thrusting through the busy day—Seldom do we taste the joy of lingering by the way—to watch a sunset or a cloud, to ponder or to pray—Yet it seems we never lack a moment just to say, what's the time?

It is always time for taking stock—Swiftly fly the minutes round the clock—But when you ask the hour you get a shock—that makes the world around you seem to rock: what's the time?

Never fail your life to rearrange—taking in things beautiful and strange—Spare a second to absorb the view—that draws your thoughts away into the blue—over the hedge beyond the garden gate—Make sure it's not too early or too late. What's the time?

Did You Not See?

The clock of life is fast and overwound. Where do you think you're going? Whither bound? . . . Slow down—ease up. Rest heart and nerves and brain. Foolish traveller, what do you hope to gain?

The world's a lovely place Did you not know? Have you not stood and watched a brooklet flow—under the arches of a willow tree? That white swan gliding by . . . did you not see?

Autumn

The first faint hint of what is yet to be—a pinkish tint upon the cherry tree—The old Virginia creepers turning red around the timbers of the garden shed—Lovely in its dying, yet how beautiful—September's golden leaves: the autumn miracle.

As sure as clocks and calendars—the year when growing old—cloaks the woods in glory—bronze, crimson, amber, gold—The fires of Nature's making, the flames no man can stay: the mighty conflagration that runs from day to day—Like torches blaze the branches in wood and garden bower—September fades but not before it lives its finest hour.

Time, Never Resting

*T*ime, never resting, works on day and night—No-one can hoard it or hinder its flight—working at healing the wounding of grief—doing its work of repair and relief.

Time's gentle touches make well and make whole—the ravage of life in the mind and the soul. Working unceasingly at its own pace—a pace all must follow, no step to retrace . . . But time is the friend of the one who can see—the blessings to come in the time yet to be.

The Tree Of Christmas

Where Autumn's red and golden ways—merge into a wintry haze—There stands, star bright, for all to see: the wonder of the Christmas tree.

The tree that year by year is lit that man may have the joy of it—and rest from turmoil, sin and strife—under the boughs of the Tree of Life: the tree of peace for all spread wide—rooted in love at Christmastide.

WARTIME
RELATIONSHIPS

Many a long cherished wartime relationship has lasted a life time. A danger shared is one that can seldom be forgotten for its roots run deep in the soil of everlasting memories.

Such memories are part of our wartime inheritance, sometimes masked in humour, a traditionally British device for disguising anything that might be mistaken for sentimentality.

Ours Is A Tale

*O*urs is a tale that shall be told by generations yet to be. Ours is a tale of battles fought through valleys of adversity. Ours is a tale of golden deeds and marvels wrought in blood and tears. Ours is a tale that will outlast the epics of a thousand years.

Write it upon the scrolls of glory. Carve it in marble, bronze and stone. This is the measure of our greatness. Let the long saga now be known . . . Lest in the future men should fail to hold these things in memory—and our sons forget the price that Britain paid for liberty.

A Handful Of Earth

*T*he soldier knelt upon the ground and sifted through his hand—a crumbling clod of German earth; a fragment of the land—that had bred the marching hosts who, flushed with pride and hate—had trampled France and stood triumphant at the Channel gate.

A tear fell on the alien dust. A glad and grateful prayer—surged up in his heart as he remembered, kneeling there—English earth; the Oxford lawns; the fens; the Devon loam. Dorset pastures, Kentish orchards, Shakespeare's meadows. Home.

The House Of Peace

We must build the house of peace on broad foundations, strong and sure—if the things we hold most precious are to stand and to endure . . . Not false friendships of old foes, but friendships proven by the years. Born of blood and agony, of sacrifice and toil and tears.

Let us keep in memory the friendships forged in war's red flame; the friendships of the battlefield, and all who fought in freedom's name . . . Let us not forget old comrades when the sounds of warfare cease. Let us build on these foundations when we build the House of Peace.

They Who Died

*T*hey have fallen into step with the immortal Dead. They have joined their comrades and are marching on ahead.

Marching to a goal that lies beyond our mortal sight, Marching to the drums of Heaven, out into the light. They who died in Italy and on the desert plains, on convoy routes to Russia, London streets and Norman lanes,

And still they come, an unseen host, to swell the company, of those who perished in the fight by land and air and sea.

In Passing

*H*e fell upon the field of battle as his boy was born, and did not live to see the coming of that happy dawn . . . Through the secret Gates of Death he left this troubled earth—as the new soul entered by the mystery of birth.

Did they come together at the Gates of Life and Death? Just before the wondrous moment of the babe's first breath—Was there an encounter? Did he touch the tiny hand? Did they meet in passing as they crossed the Borderland?

This Be Their Epitaph

*F*rom the clean hands of the young we take the gift supreme: the gift of life and liberty, the right to work and dream . . . We take what they have won for us: a thing above all price. What do we offer in return for that high sacrifice?

They have served their generation—wise beyond their years—Following their Star of faith through mud and blood and tears . . . We shall remember, though once more we learn to live and laugh. They were the saviours of the world . . . This be their epitaph.

Wartime Friendships

As we make our journey down the winding road of War—We cannot linger very long at Friendship's lighted door . . . We lift the latch and cross the threshold, but we cannot stay. We exchange a greeting and we pass upon our way.

Many fellow-travellers along the road we hail—We fall in step, then off we go along another trail . . . with our wartime friends we part—for so it has to be. But their names are written in the book of memory.

The Fairest Sight In All The World

Silver-winged above the earth men travel through the sky. We are told that in the future everyone will fly—But we, who are an island race, must not forget the sea. Ships have made us what we are and shaped our destiny.

Ships! . . . The magic word evokes the thought of wind and tide—Docks and harbours, blue horizons, oceans deep and wide—Mighty vessels bound for lands romantic and remote. The fairest sight in all the world: a lovely ship afloat.

Under Orders

*I*f every soldier in the field his course of action planned—If none obeyed the orders issued by the high command, no victory could be achieved, for chaos would be rife. So it is with all who fight the battle we call Life.

We are under orders. God's commands we must obey—Taking not the road we'd choose, but His appointed way . . . Life's an endless warfare; evil sleeps not day or night. We'd rather live at peace, but we are ordered to the fight.

FAMILY TIES

One way or another your life from its beginning is shaped by the depth or shallowness of family roots. Even if you have no children of your own you have ties through a brother, sister, mother or grandmother, father or grandfather, cousins, aunts and uncles. Lonely indeed must be the soul who can lay no claim to ties with anyone. A brother in Timbuctoo or a second cousin who married a South African at the other end of the world go to the forming of blood links. Even if these persons are never or rarely seen, they verify your claim of belonging to a family.

Partners

*T*he first dance of all when they danced heart to heart—they knew, they both knew, it was only the start—of something more wonderful than a mere dance—more than a thrill of a passing romance.

They knew without saying that Love, the real thing—had touched them that night with its shimmering wing. No word had been spoken and yet they both knew—that suddenly all sorts of dreams had come true.

It's many a year since the night that they met— but that first dance they will never forget . . . Then boy and girl and now husband and wife— still happy, still dancing, and partners for life.

From The Family

*M*ore than you think we miss you. More than words can tell. We're sending you this message—hoping you'll soon be well . . . Life's not the same without you. The waiting seems so long. So hurry up—Get better—and come back well and strong.

More than you guess you're wanted. More often than you know—our thoughts and prayers are with you—because we love you so . . . Be patient, brave and hopeful. Have faith and you will see—that God will work the wonder. "The best is yet to be".

Christmas Thoughts

*A*ll the world is young on Christmas Day. Our grown-up worries seem to melt away. There is a feeling that we can't explain—for we become like children once again.

The faith of childhood springs in us anew. Our hearts grow lighter, brighter, warmer too. And life takes on a sweet simplicity. God comes so close—not veiled in mystery—But as a child; a small and helpless thing. The baby Christ, the little Saviour-King. This is the thought that breaks down human pride—the tender thought that comes at Christmastide.

To Live For Always In My Heart

*L*ooking back in memory a baby I recall—the centre of our universe, the dearest thing of all. Next I see a toddler, then a child with laughing eyes. Now a girl engaged to marry . . . Goodness how Time flies!

Soon she'll be a bride and I am wanting her to know—I'm happy in her happiness. The children have to go—and make their own homes somewhere else. It can't be otherwise—but on her wedding day when we have kissed and said goodbyes—the little girl of yesterday will stay behind with me—to live for always in my heart: the child of memory.

The Parlour

We talk about the drawing-room, the lounge, the dining-nook. But I prefer the parlour with its prim and formal look. The word suggests a room that has a Sunday atmosphere—a place where switched-on voices cannot jar upon the ear.

A room for conversation and for sewing thoughtfully—where a woman can enjoy a quiet cup of tea . . . A room of charm and character with curtains crisp and bright—flowery covers on the chairs and paintwork shining white.

The modern home is full of gadgets, comfort, luxury. Customs change and fashions alter. So it has to be . . . Old words pass from use, new words take their place somehow—but what a pity no one seems to have a 'parlour' now!

The Bridges Of The Years

*B*irthdays are like bridges that you cross from year to year: bridges on the road of Time. Old landmarks disappear—as you take the unknown path that lies ahead of you. The end of it is hidden, the horizon veiled from view.

There'll be hills to climb. It can't be easy all the way—with roses everywhere you go and sunshine every day—but cross your bridges hopefully, believing in the best. Face with faith whatever comes and truly you'll be blessed.

Hoping Somebody Would Call

Don't let anyone be lonely in your village or your town. Time erects its barriers, so do your best to break them down—before too many days go by, too many months, too many years . . . Risk a snub and make a gesture. Use your eyes and use your ears—to find out who's in need of friendship and a bit of company. It's the duty of a Christian to be kind and neighbourly.

Sometimes someone dies or to a hospital is sent away. Circumstances come to light and then too late you hear them say—We never knew that there was someone living near in such distress— hoping somebody would call to ease the ache of loneliness.

The Eyes Of A Child

Lovely are the eyes of children, angel-pure and starry bright. Happy, guileless, trusting, candid—shining with the inner light of the uncorrupted mind, by wordly wisdom undefiled. Speak no word to cast a shadow on the clear eyes of a child.

With foolish and indecent haste we force the pace of growth and so—too soon they lose that shining look. Too soon they learn, too soon they grow—Too soon comes knowledge of wrong-doing, sex and vice and violence. Let them be children. Cut not short the springtime of their innocence.

You Pass But Once

*O*nce, only once, you pass along this way. So do the good you mean to do each day . . . If it's worthwhile—it's risky to delay. Tomorrow? What may happen? Who can say?

Those well known lines in many a home you see. A little jewel of philosophy . . . "You pass but once". Your opportunity—is now and here, wherever you may be.

We pass but once! How true those words remain! We're all on the move. We call time back in vain . . . Do not let that good intention wane— because you will not pass this way again.

The Homeward Journey

One road winds over the mountains through storm clouds wild and cold—another runs out to the sunset in a glory of crimson and gold . . . Some go by way of green pastures where the healing waters spring—refreshing the soul that has travelled deep valleys of suffering.

Good is the road that leads forward to comfort, contentment and rest—and good is the road of adventure pursuing an unending quest—but there is a point of convergence—where my road meets your road, my friend—for we're all on the same homeward journey, and all roads are one in the end.

Let's Begin

Let's begin—Yes, let's begin—with the broken threads of our dreams to spin—a shroud to bury the past away—weaving a new dream for today . . . Resolved to make our marriage work—No effort spare, no duty shirk—Forgiving, forgetting the hurtful thing—To life's many problems new wisdom bring.

Remember that wonderful wedding day? Of course, you do. So let us say—No more quarrelling, no more strife—Come to terms with love and life—behaving well through thick and thin—best and worst . . . Come, let's begin.

LEARNING TO WAIT

Some people are so busy picking up burdens that they forget to look at the date on the label. All too often the burden they think they have to bear today turns out to be the one marked "For Tomorrow". Once you catch up with the folk who are over-anxious to overtake tomorrow you will soon find yourself in a crowd. Far too many people are in this kind of a hurry. Beware of forming a relationship with anyone impatiently anticipating trouble. You'll find yourself being carried along against your will. Learn to wait for what you don't really want. Some unwanted burdens disappear before you can pick them up.

Push Back The Horizon

*P*ush back the horizon. Allow no cloud to bar—your passage to the future. Go forward and go far . . . Ignore the flimsy curtain that floats beyond your view. Never allow horizons to halt or hinder you . . . Force them ever backwards into empty space. Fear no deceptive barriers. They're nothing but mist and lace. Tomorrow calls and beckons. Your star is guiding you. Sail on and trust the Captain to take and bring you through.

The Dreamers

*D*reamers can't keep up with those who walk the quickest pace—They like to stroll, while others rush to win life's hectic race . . . Folks who push the rest aside, the hustling bustling kind— forge ahead and seem to leave the dreamers far behind.

But the dreamer sees a lot the other fellows miss—He has time to look around—to feel the sun's warm kiss—Time to watch and time to wonder, pausing here and there—Time to pray and time to ponder, time to stand and stare.

Oftentimes the hustlers flag before they reach their goal—having no resources left of body, brain or soul . . . And the dreamer overtakes them, ambling gaily past—Having come the long slow way, he gets there at the last.

Look For The Best

Look for the best and not the worst in everyone you meet—the friend who knocks upon your door, the stranger in the street . . . Look for the beauty not the flaws in every character—the good intention not the bad, the kindness, not the slur.

Close an eye to faults and failings. You have failings too. Pray that God will do the same and not be hard on you—noting your redeeming points, and not remembering every little weakness in the day of reckoning.

That's our only hope of coming through the final test—the hope that we'll be judged not by the worst but by the best . . . If the Lord ignored our virtues, seeing just the vice—Who would ever get beyond the gates of Paradise?

Seek Ye First

Where to find direction in the chaos all around? That's the question. Where can peace and happiness be found? . . . How can one pursue the high and finer things of life—when the world is torn with hatreds, selfishness and strife?

Seek ye first God's Kingdom. Other guests are all in vain—bringing disappointment and frustration in their train—if we have not sought and found the thing beyond all price: the Truth the Master came to teach through love and sacrifice.

Seek ye first this precious pearl—before all other things—Nothing else will satisfy or give the spirit wings—to rise above despair and with a faith triumphant face—the evils and the ills that now beset the human race.

Greet The New

Let the Old Year pass away. Mourn not but greet the New. Turn your eyes in hope and faith towards the distant view . . . Know that you'll be guided safely down the unmapped road—given strength and courage for the bearing of your load.

Do not let the unknown future fill you with dismay. It is in the hands of God—so go upon your way. Trust in Him and have no fear. You do not walk alone. He leads the faithful in the dark and careth for His own.

Leave behind your grievances, your worry and your woe. Drop the extra burden of your grudges . . . Let them go—so that you can travel lighter with a conscience clear—Out into the great adventure of another year.

Voices

The weakling says, "I'm beaten", but the fighter says, "Not I." The shirker says it can't be done, the worker says, "I'll try." . . . The laggard says he's weary and must drop out of the race. The plodder says, "Keep going at a good and steady pace."

The pessimist, when clouds appear, predicts a rainy day. The optimist declares he sees a gold streak in the grey . . . The grumbler says he's sick of life; work, sleep, the dull routine. The poet says, "The stars still shine, birds sing and grass is green."

The cynic says this crazy world is rushing to its doom. The dreamer cries, "I see the peaks of glory through the gloom." . . . The doubter asks, "Where now is God? No sign do we perceive"— and someone at a cross is kneeling, saying, "I believe."

Wayside Glory

*H*e who walks with seeing eyes along a country lane—now beholds the wayside hedges glorified again . . . Garlanded in vernal green, the twigs once black and bare—lift their rosy coronals into the fragrant air.

Buttercups and bittersweet upon the banks in bloom—underneath the shining fountains of the yellow broom . . . Foam of blossom on the thorn and scents upon the breeze. Gold of gorse and flags of fern around the leafing trees.

Cottage gardens, deep in lilac, greet the passer-by—damson, quince and appleblow delighting heart and eye . . . Happy is the wanderer whose feet unhurried stray—down the lanes of England in the lovely month of May.

Worship

*A*ll around us now we see dissension and dismay. This is what the world becomes when men no longer pray. Fear and hunger stalk the earth, suspicion, greed and strife. This is what the modern creeds have made of human life.

Walk again the quiet ways of faith and charity. Worship Him Who made the earth, the sun, the stars, the sea—God the Father and Creator, Love supreme, sublime—Lord of life and death, of men and angels, space and time.

Let us then to God's own House return with prayer and praise—asking Him to guide us through the dark and troubled days . . . To restore the broken nations and the whole world bless—leading us along the paths of peace and righteousness.

Something In The Heart

*T*here is something in the heart that keeps us strong and sane—in the hour of peril, of temptation and of pain—Bids us cling to life in spite of sorrow and of loss—pointing to the light behind the shadow of the cross.

There is something in the soul that yearns to spread its wings—with the wild desire to breathe the breath of higher things—something that abhors all evil, ugliness and strife—and responds to truth and goodness, beauty, love and life.

Underneath the outward show of personality—lies the holy part of us that lives eternally—This spiritual consciousness that no man can define—that changes human nature with a touch of the divine.

Tomorrow's Burden

*D*on't pick up Tomorrow's burden while it's still Today. Hour by hour we're given strength our part in life to play—Light sufficient to illume the path that we must tread—Not enough to pierce the darkness of the miles ahead . . .

We in some mysterious way are helped when things go wrong—Shoulders stoop beneath the strain—and yet we get along—finding that we have the power to meet each fresh demand—if we reach out in the dark and hold the unseen Hand.

Never look for storms approaching when the skies you scan. Don't anticipate the future; it's not ours to plan. Do not strain your eyes to see the turnings in the road. Why take on before you must another extra load?

Don't go searching down the byways for the things you fear. There's no need to fight the next day's battle till you hear—the summons of the trumpet and the beating of the drums. Don't pick up Tomorrow's burden till Tomorrow comes.

A Change Of Heart

Yesterday's steps you can't retrace—by slowing down or quickening pace—changing course, or turning back—You still will be on the same old track—The only change worthwhile you'll find—will be a change of heart and mind—leading and directing you—on towards that lovely view.

Keep to the rules and bear your load—along the rough and rutted road—on that wayside seat awhile—gathering strength for the second mile—Keeping an eye on the distant height—that draws you on by day and night—walking tall and walking straight—the better world to recreate.

Upside Down

*U*pside down and inside out this mad world seems today—When you come to think of it you know not what to say—Are we crazy rushing on along the road to doom—never caring where we're going, never making room—for sober thoughts that lead away from never-ending strife—towards the pastures of a more enlightened mode of life.

Did no-one ever warn us and has no-one ever heard—the voice that in the silence speaks the Everlasting Word?—Blind and deaf and ignorant, this voice we failed to heed—pathetic now we stand unguarded in our hour of need—clutching at a reed to keep afloat and keep alive—the Bible to restore, to resurrect and to revive.

Never Say No

Never say No to Hope, when Hope comes knocking at the door—to bid you look ahead, towards the happier days in store—Never say No to Hope when Hope comes dancing down your way—with something great to communicate, and something good to say.

Never refuse to listen, for she brings a word for you—bidding you take the upward slope that commands the broadest view—But Hope is always in a hurry brooking no delay—So never say No when Hope calls out—Come take the high way, MY way.

ALL CREATURES
GREAT AND SMALL

There is a sense in which we are all related to one another within the common framework of humanity, but that does not mean we are all alike in every way. The Creator in his infinite wisdom divided the world into separate races each with its own spiritual and physical possibilities and limitations. As they were all created may they all remain, each respecting the purity of his own race bound only by the things which unify and bless "all creatures that on earth do dwell."

We Cannot Always Understand

We cannot always understand why this or that should be. The picture Time is working out upon the tapestry is hidden on the other side and no one can explain the meaning of the heart-ache and the anguish and the pain.

Perhaps we never shall be told. Perhaps we'll never know. Faith must be sufficient as upon our way we go, never asking why hopes turned to ashes, joy to tears—believing that beyond the little measure of the years, we shall see the reason for the thing we suffered here. The answer will be given and God's purposes made clear.

All Our Days Are Numbered

*A*ll our days are numbered but it's not for us to know—just how many days are left. So don't let this one go—unmarked by something good or lovely, something true or fine—something that redeems it with a touch of the divine.

Think a thought that lifts your mind on to a higher track. Do the thing that takes a load from someone else's back . . . Say the word that changes conflict into harmony. Strike the note that turns the discord into melody.

Take this day out of its groove. Before you let it go—Give to it a meaning and a glory. Let it glow! There are many little ways in which it's possible—to sanctify the commonplace and make it beautiful.

Love Is A Solvent

Love is a solvent. Love dissolves a heart as hard as stone. By a secret alchemy—by ways and means unknown—love works wonders—changing people, shaping lives anew—focusing a kindly light upon a hopeless view.

Love is a solvent. Love breaks up resentments firmly set. Love is the power that helps us to forgive and to forget—the grievances that rankle. Thoughts that hurt and things that smart. Love is the solvent that dissolves the hardness of the heart.

Christmas Is For Everyone

Christmas is for everyone for Christmas is for sharing—the joys, the blessings and the burdens. Christmas is for caring—putting into practice what the Saviour came to prove: that life is good when hearts are moved by kindness and by love.

Christmas is for everyone for Christmas is for spreading—the happy news from Bethlehem, the light of heaven shedding—on the vicious and the vile, the evil and the wrong. Christmas bids us stand and listen to the angel's song.

Christmas is for everyone; for every race and nation—bringing hope and happiness, redemption and salvation. Not for Christmas only but for all the world to see—God appearing in the vesture of humanity.

The Command

*P*eace! Be still—the Master said. We tend to think that He—spoke in soft and gentle manner—speaking tenderly—but was not this imperative, a definite command, a sharp rebuke to those who could not grasp or understand the meaning of the truths that He had come here to declare? Stop worrying. He says to us. Stop rushing here and there. Stop arguing. Stop quarrelling—and be not torn apart. Let the Word of God be heard within the quiet heart.

In this age of strife and noise and turmoil we today—need to listen for that voice—to hear and to obey . . . above the voices of the world that clamour hard and shrill—He speaks with calm authority, commanding Peace—Be still!

The Precious Portion

Do not think of life in terms of trial and tragedy, but simply as a tiny fragment of Eternity where we catch the echoed music of unfinished themes and strive with broken threads to work the tapestry of dreams.

In this world of change and chance we cannot hope to see the meanings and the purposes behind the mystery. Here we make beginnings but we cannot see the ends. Well contented we should be if when the dark descends, we can offer a thanksgiving unto One above for the blessings of the years: the happiness, the love, the precious portion granted. Let the rest be cast aside. Remember what a good God gave and not what was denied.

Heaven

*H*eaven is love made perfect within God's gracious plan. Heaven is love completed beyond life's little span. Heaven is love's true homeland where kindred souls abide—where death has no dominion and nothing can divide.

Heaven is love's tomorrow, unmarred by doubt or fear. Heaven is where we harvest the seed we scatter here. Heaven is love's fulfilling the promises made good—of all that we have dreamed of but never understood.

Nine Times Out Of Ten

Nine time out of ten life seems to work out for the best. Nine times out of ten you find that if you let things rest—Providence will sort them out without your helping hand—Not perhaps exactly in the way that you had planned—but in a wiser way and from a broader point of view. So do not try to force events or push your own plans through . . . Cease to worry. Trust and pray. Though things look black as night—Nine times out of ten you find that everything comes right.

Follow Me

Never heed the sceptics or the cynics who deny—truths that have withstood the storms of ages rolling by . . . They who doubt the Word of God have nothing to replace—the wisdom, the philosophy, the glory and the grace—of the Truth proclaimed to man in little Galilee—Valid for the passing needs of every century.

Times may change as change they must, but Truth can never be—subject to the fads and fashions of humanity . . . Truth eternal shines above the turmoil and the strife—in the form of One who was Himself the Way, the Life.

None before or since has said the things He came to say. He spoke for future generations and for this, our day . . . when He taught upon the hills and preached beside the sea—the simple gospel of the Kingdom saying, Follow Me.

Under The Shadow Of A Guiding Hand

We do not always see the way ahead. We do not always know which path to tread. This is the point at which we need to light the lamp of Faith to take into the night.

Trust and believe that God is leading you to a fulfilment hidden from your view. Know only good can come of what is planned, under the shadow of that guiding Hand.

It is not always granted us to see what lies behind the present mystery. Waste not your words in asking why or where. Time will unfold the answer to your prayer.

All Things New

Newness of life may the New Year bring—New life for every living thing—Man and beast and soil and tree—languish in their impurity . . . The earth is sick and sour and old—The world's long tale is all but told—but the Leader rides on through the storm and the strife—saying, "I am the Way, the Truth and the Life."

We who are willing lost paths to retrace—how can we rescue the whole human race? We, the believers, how can we restore—the faithless, the hopeless who cry at the door? . . . The promise still holds and the promise is true—"Behold," said the Lord, "I make everything new."

QUIET TIMES

Quietude is not a frilling to mental composure. It is a necessity. Unless the mind is at ease it cannot make contact with that other world which is the fountain of all inspiration.

Echoes In A Quiet Room

I sit in a web of shadows—and the clock in sleepy mood—wakens the sense of magic that comes with solitude . . . I hear—or I dream I'm hearing beyond its fairy chimes—the echo of lost enchantments, and music of gracious times.

The whisper of silks and satins. The tones of an old spinet. The footsteps of stately figures, dancing a minuet . . . The tinkle of crystal glasses. The laughter, like silver bells. The voices as soft and lovely as murmur of waves in shells.

The swish of a fan unfolding. The clink of a jewelled chain. You ask is it fact or fancy. The mystery must remain . . . I and the clock know the answer, but the secret we must keep. We know what we hear in the stillness when the old house falls asleep.

The Quiet Ways

*W*hether you are sitting by a well, wandering round an old church or walking in deep lanes you are going in the right direction if it is peace you are seeking. We do not realise it because we live in a bedlam of noise these days, but deep inside we are all longing for peace because we have lost it. There is something within that is crying out for quietness because we need it. You are not alone in this desperate need. At every turn you will meet one with whom you can claim a relationship. Life on its present levels degrades us. Join then the ranks of those who are going about in this depraved world hungry for a peace that is a spiritual food for famished souls.

Down In The Secret Garden

Year by year the blackbird comes the April nest to build. Year by year the little sunken garden here is filled—with liquid notes that rise and fall like fountains through the trees—in a jet of silvery music blowing on the breeze.

Deep below the street it lies, this narrow walled-in place—and upon the moss green stones the shadows interlace—when boughs of apple and of lilac in the wind are stirred . . . Year by year it comes, the magic fluting of this bird—down there in the secret garden somewhere out of sight—in the morning glory and the mellow evening light.

Lost In A Crowd

When many faces I can see—I'm lost in multiplicity. And losing my identity I ask in terror, Where is me? The I that hides in flesh and bone—is blind and deaf when not alone.

When many voices can be heard—crescendo, rising word on word—I cannot hear the voice that calls—in solitude when silence falls . . . For only there is wholeness found—beyond the range of sight and sound—the integrated self is free—to come and go, to hear and see.

The Day Of The Pearl

Now, and then you live a day outside the daily round—Chains are loosed, old concepts die, a different world is found—New dimensions open, joy is glimpsed, perfection seen—Like a peep of paradise flashed out upon a screen.

You were given eyes to see and thoughts to understand—Someone else's self-made garden wonderfully planned—Woke a sleeping dream in you that will forever be—Like a pearl encapsulated in a memory.

Go With The Flow

Go with the flow of Providence wherever that may be. Go with the current that knows its way into the open sea . . . Don't stand about on the brink of life afraid to venture in. Go with the flow of circumstances. Follow the voice within.

Go where God wills although it leads to stress and turbulence—Go with the driving of the wind that moves the day's events . . . Go where you're driven. Trust the hand that will not let you go—pulled by the tides, you know not where, but going with the flow.

Be Still And Listen

*H*ow can He come to an unquiet mind? How show His face to the inwardly blind? How can a sense of His presence be caught—in the confusion of turbulent thought?

If you would savour the calm of that peace—stop, wait and listen. Let questionings cease. Sit in the silence. Be still and believe—that you at His hands a great gift will receive—of healing and blessing . . . Doubt not He will come—as once to the lame and the deaf and the dumb—He came with new life—to revive and restore. Make ready your heart for He stands at the door.

Sit By The Well

Crowds had thronged with their demands—eager for those healing hands—and so when evening shadows fell—the Master came to Jacob's Well—to sit awhile and to refresh—the weariness of mind and flesh.

If He, the Lord, desired to rest—we too when troubled and hard-pressed—should learn of Him and drop the load—to rest awhile beside the road.

Sit by the well. You've travelled far. There is no well? Then where you are—Repose in Him that you might live—and living water He will give—your thirst to quench when strength has gone. Replenished, you can travel on.

Take Your Time

*T*ake your time—or time takes you and drains your strength away. Take a minute, maybe two, throughout your busy day—for slowing down to meditate—from wordly things apart—in a quiet place to wait with a receptive heart. Take your time to think about the greatest things of all—take your time to work it out before the curtains fall.

Why the worry? What's the hurry? Take your time and stroll—picking from life's wayside hedges that which feeds the soul . . . Take your time and walk on grass; to look at flowers and trees—wandering and pondering on wonders such as these . . . Slacken pace to see the view. Take your time or time takes you.

Believing

*D*on't go round looking for sympathy, displaying your weakness for others to see . . . Trust not on luck, it's a trick and a fake—but build up a spirit that nothing can break.

Believe in yourself and the Other who's there—Holding you close in His own special care . . . Face every day with clean hands and clean slate. It's never too soon and it's never too late. To shoulder your burden and make a new start— with a song in your soul and a hope in your heart.

The Right Word For Today

When you feel frustrated, helpless and distraught—with the many battles that daily must be fought—Quietly sit and lower your rope into the well—of life that is as high as heaven and as deep as hell.

Each must draw his bucket of water, foul or pure—each must choose things good or evil, flimsy or secure—Each must make his choice: Life's law to flout or to obey—to be dumb or to proclaim the right word for today.

A GOOD NEIGHBOUR

Fortunate are you if you know what it is to have a good neighbour. Fortunate indeed if you can go away for a long time or a little secure in the knowledge that there is someone next door who will keep a watchful eye on cat, garden, and property while you are away. If you have a good neighbour you are on the way to having a good friend.

Neighbour and Friend

She watches when she knows that there is nobody about. She wonders when strangers click the gate, passing in and out . . . She keeps a caring eye on things; concerned, she is aware—of anyone or everyone who has no business there.

Conscious of her duty as a neighbour, standing guard—Observing the comings and goings from a window or a yard.

Fortunate are they in whom these two great virtues blend—the capacity of being both a neighbour and a friend.

Let Hope Go Ahead

*L*et Hope go ahead and you follow. Let Hope go before you today. Things will be better tomorrow if Hope be in view all the way—for Hope bears no load on her shoulders—Smoothing the rocks and the ruts—she forces a path through the boulders, dismissing the ifs and the buts.

You won't be afraid to keep going—where Hope sheds a gleam on the track—for Hope with her lamp brightly glowing—moves forward and never turns back . . . she never needs goading or prodding—unflagging she makes for the height—while you in her footprints come plodding—eyes fixed on her beautiful light.

Alone you would soon give up trying. Alone you would never succeed—but Hope undismayed and undying—strides forward to give you a lead . . . And now that a new year is dawning—and unknown the road you must tread—There's nothing to fear if each morning—you're willing to send Hope ahead.

So Little

The gentle smile, the reconciling touch—can cost so little and can mean so much—to heal a breach or mend a friendship broken—a letter written, or a sentence spoken.

What hurts and pangs we suffer needlessly! What pains inflict, because we cannot see—how much we lose through conflicts and contentions—poisoning life with quarrels and dissensions.

Let them all go and love triumphant be—over all evil, hate, greed, jealously . . . Love's tender word, forbearing and forgiving—brings to the heart true peace and joy of living.

Time Steps Out

*T*ime is slow when we are young, but as the years proceed—Time steps out and seems to move at twice its former speed . . . Swiftly are the milestones passed—we see them flashing by— Quickly do the birthdays come—Time races . . . seasons fly.

Do not bank upon the future—It's not yours to plan—No one but your Maker knows the measure of your span . . . We should always live each day as if it were the last—the only chance to make amends for failings of the past.

The Backlash

Nature always lashes back. Man never really wins—so we have to pay the price for all the many sins—of ignorance and arrogance that we commit each day—all because we will not live the good, the simple way.

We pollute the rivers and contaminate the seas—and with deadly poisons spread the earth and spray the trees—We create obnoxious waste and dump it anywhere. We make fumes that load with death the sweetness of the air.

Faster we desire to turn the wheels of industry—in the sacred name of progress and prosperity—Let us learn before our follies bring on us the curse—of Him whose everlasting laws sustain the universe.

Three Days

*T*hree days and three days only are really your concern—So drop the futile worries and let the seasons turn . . . Three days! You'll find it simpler reducing things this way—to yesterday, tomorrow and the present day.

The first you cannot alter for yesterday has gone—and though regrets still linger you have to carry on—praying for forgiveness—There's nothing else to do—to banish the remembrance of all that troubles you.

Tomorrow is a secret. The far horizon's rim—conceals God's hidden purpose—so leave it all with Him. Today's the day that matters. Today is yours to live—So take it and be grateful for what it has to give.

Too many

*T*oo many people—too many crowds—too many babies born. Too many houses where there should be—cattle and crops and corn . . . Too many voices—seldom a pause—making a restful space. Too many noises jarring the ear. Never a quiet place.

Too many smashes—too many cars. Not enough time to reflect. Too many clashes—too many words. Too many marriages wrecked . . . Too many homes where Love is left out. Homes rich and poor where you see—selfishness, cruelty, strife, discontent. Hell where a heaven should be.

This is our world as created by man—Man who has marred the original plan—spoiling the earth that the Saviour once trod—trying and failing to live without God.

The Kindred Spirits

Kindred spirits meet unsought—By the alchemy of thought. Towards each other they are led—guided by the unseen thread—of accident or passing chance—caught in webs of circumstance.

Kindred spirits, souls in tune—come together late or soon—like notes that harmonize when played. Thus true marriages are made—and lifelong friendships come about. Time alone can work it out.

Surely there must be a force—behind all human intercourse—weaving lives through chance and change—the perfect pattern to arrange—so two in tune at last will meet—knowing life to be complete.

Pick and Choose

*P*ick and choose between the thoughts that throng around your mind. Some are good and some are bad, some happy, some unkind. But it's up to you to say which ones you'll entertain of the many thoughts that seek admittance to your brain . . . And remember thoughts have power to heal or to destroy—turning heaven into hell or sorrow into joy.

Thoughts can change life's colour, mould your face and change your views—so be careful what you think. You're free to pick and choose—so choose a good thought for the day, a thought to carry you—through the many problems that are bound to get at you—out there in the world where all is turmoil, strain and stress—Yours the choice so choose the best. Choose peace, choose happiness.

Things Change

When you get to the end of your tether—and your energy seems to have gone—When you're weary and wondering whether its worth while to keep struggling on—When the fire has gone out of your spirit—and your armour has fallen apart—Let go and let God do the fighting. Be still in your head and your heart.

When the music goes out of the morning and you cannot keep pace with the drum—When the flowers in the garden stop smiling—and the birds do not sing when you come . . . When the sun never peeps through your window and you look for the rainbow in vain—Ask someone to help and to heal you. Let Him take the brunt and the strain.

When you get to the end of your courage—and there's nothing much more you can do—Try folding your hands for a moment and letting God's guidance get through . . . Life can't be altered by worry. Stop trying to push it your way. Just let the good Lord take over. You'll find that things change when you pray.

Rich Man's Fare, But Table Bare

You can't afford this and you can't afford that—The bills must come first so you can't have the hat . . . That's life as we know it. You can't keep afloat—but remember your neighbour is in the same boat.

When we were young we weren't scrambling to reach—the top of the tree for the pear or the peach. We did not fight for the sweetest and best—grateful we were for the least we possessed.

That's why the children grow up as they do—not taught to look for the good and the true . . . Teachers and parents the guilt now must share—for leaving the children a table that's bare.

THE SPECIAL
FRIEND

*Sometimes in the course of life a mere
relationship can ripen into real friendship.
It can happen in a day or after a long period
of time, but you will know when it has
come. Your heart will tell you.*

The Keynote

A tuning fork will strike the note from which you take the key—for the making of the music of the melody . . . It cannot sound a range of tones and semi-tones for you. One note and one alone it strikes, but that one note is true.

Love is like a tuning fork that gives the note we need—for making life harmonious in thought and word and deed: the note we have to strike before we find the magic key—in which to play the music of the daily symphony: the symphony of living: blended themes that rise and fall. Sweet the sound if Love be found, the keynote of it all.

Time Was Kinder Than I Thought

*T*ime was kinder than I thought, the many changes that it wrought and the sorrows that it brought, proved at last beneficent. Time indeed was provident.

Much it took but much remained. Much was lost but more was gained. In ways that never were explained, the burden lifted from my back, the mountain moved, the cloud rolled back.

The dream that seemed impossible came true as by a miracle, through happenings most wonderful—I found the blessing that I sought . . . Time was kinder than I thought.

The New

*T*he New is here at your very door demanding to come in. You have heard it knocking. You have barred yourself within—and you have refused to answer. But the New is here bringing tomorrow, bringing the future, bringing another year.

A stranger, yes, but one with claims that cannot be denied, one you dare not leave unheeded in the dark outside, one to whom some day, somewhere, a hand you must extend, one who in the course of time may prove to be a friend.

Lord, This Day I Need Thee

Lord, this is a special time for me. And more than human love and sympathy—I need the comfort of the consciousness—that Thou art nigh to strengthen and to bless.

Lord, I've never come this way before. I need Thy Word my courage to restore . . . I need Thy hand to reach for fearlessly—in the ordeal that lies ahead of me.

Now in my weakness, Lord, I need so much— the balm and the blessing of Thy healing touch . . . Thee I have failed—and yet I dare to say—Be Thou my Friend and meet my need this day.

That Is What It Means To Have A Friend

*S*omeone to tell your troubles to when troubles come along. Someone with whom to talk things over when they're going wrong. A prayer to say, a smile to give, a helping hand to lend— that is what it means to have a friend.

Someone to reinforce your courage when it starts to flag. Someone to ease the burden when the spine begins to sag. Someone to keep you going when a mountain you ascend—that is what it means to have a friend.

Someone to share the problem and to help you work it out. Somebody to confide in when assailed by fear or doubt. Someone to give you back your faith when hope comes to an end—that is what it means to have a friend.

Nobody knows

Nobody knows what a prayer can do—when somebody, somewhere, prays for you. Burdens are lifted and doors unbarred. Nothing seems quite so bad or hard.

Nobody knows how God intervenes—working His wonders behind the scenes, turning the evil away from us, in a way most marvellous.

Clearing a path through the tangled track. Easing the strain on the breaking back. When Hope fades away and is lost to view—Nobody knows what a prayer will do.

Every Day, Every Year

You need every friend you can make—in a world where things hurt, and hearts break. Friends who will always be there—the good and the bad times to share . . . But friendship two-sided must be—each giving much, yet both free—going a separate way—wherever life leads day by day.

Friendships, the new and the old—form links that connect and will hold—in spite of the day to day strain—One friendship will always remain . . . Through changes and chances you learn—To this one special friend you can turn—the friend who unchanged will appear any time—any day—any year.

Somebody Said That Somebody Said

Somebody said that somebody said. Trouble was caused and suspicion fed. Somebody passed on an idle word. Someone repeated what someone had heard.

There has been many a broken heart. Many a marriage has come apart. Many relationships have been changed. Many a neighbour become estranged. In many a home where peace once reigned affection and loyalty have been strained, and many a life is incomplete all because someone was indiscreet.

Many a friendship has been wrecked— through gossip unfounded and unchecked. Mischief was made and a rumour spread. Somebody said that somebody said.

Where Is Comfort

Who can face without defeat the worst that life can do—standing unembittered and unbroken? Who comes through—with faith undimmed the agonies of Love's most grievous loss? He who down upon his knees can look up at the Cross.

All around him others go to pieces hopelessly—underneath the bludgeonings of trial and tragedy—but they that wait upon the Lord their failing strength renew—knowing that His word is valid and his promise true . . . Where is solace?

Where is peace, the touch that cures and calms? Only in the comfort of the Everlasting Arms.

A Word Of Thanks

Words are so inadequate our feelings to convey. When the heart is full we often find it hard to say—how much we appreciate what other people do, but I hope these lines express my gratitude to you—for your friendship, for your help and for your sympathy—You will never ever know how much you've done for me . . . When I needed someone you were there to help me through—So these simple words of thanks I'd like to send to you: brief they are but truly meant—and with warm affection sent.

That Wonderful Day

*T*he wonderful day I shall never forget—That day long ago when we two met—Time stood still for a moment or two—when you saw me and I saw you.

Love at first sight. It happened thus—It happened that day and happened to us—strangers. Your name I'd never heard—We gave no sign and spoke no word.

It was nothing less than a miracle—impossible, incredible—To be in a strange and crowded place—becoming aware of a single face.

Who can explain it? Nobody—But it happened to you and it happened to me—in that first moment when we two met—on the wonderful day I shall never forget.

ODDS AND ENDS

After all, what does life consist of when all is said and done? Is it not a confusion of odds and ends, meetings and parting, failures and successes, beginnings and endings, bits and pieces. Make sure you make the most of the odds and ends that come your way. Each item has a meaning and a message, but it may take a lifetime to discover answers to the questions they raise.

Just For Fun

*T*he sun like a crimson ball bounces amongst the trees—Here in the stormy twilight it comes rushing on the breeze—through the open gaps between the branches, running wild—Slipping up and dipping down like the plaything of a child.

The sun on such a day as this gets somewhat out of hand—Instead of holding court on the horizon, grave and grand—It abandons its dignity and frolics just for fun—forgetting it is King of the sky, His Majesty the sun.

The Last Leaf

Look! Keep looking till it falls, the last leaf on the tree. When it flutters to your feet you'll know it cannot be—very long to wait until the winter's tale is told—with autumn's glory spent in piled up leaves, bronze, red and gold.

Look and keep on looking though the time you cannot spare—spare this, one moment more to stand, to wonder and to stare . . . This leaf you'll never see again; this autumn too must pass—unless reflected; given back through Memory's magic glass.

Which Way?

The season is passing by the door. So sparse is the summer's poor yield . . . The gold of the grain unharvested—lies wasted in the field.

Blame the rain. But first stand still. Consider Nature's laws. Against them all men have transgressed; so let us call a pause—and come to terms that satisfy the needs of all concerned. Things natural or mechanical? False doctrines have we learned?

The field beyond the meadow is an open book to read. Instead of sheaves the hayrick stands: a mocking joke indeed! Is this the way to treat the land? Is this the way to go—towards prosperity and peace? Ask them. They think they know.

You Know

You know that you are guided all the way. In the silence voices seem to say . . . This is the way; the only way for you. Trust it and take it, with the goal in view.

This is your road, the road of destiny. Trust and believe and protected you will be. Deep in the darkness through the night you grope—Over the hills of promise and of hope.

Keep to the track. Stray not to left or right. Keep bravely on and hold the end in sight. All will be well with Faith to point the way. There's glory ahead. Dawn ushers in the day.

That Second Chance

*E*very night that closes a day brings opportunity—to repent of the mistakes you made, and failed to see . . . At the time caught up in the confusions of the day—But now at last comes the quiet moment when you can pause to pray—for the second chance you want to do the thing that's right—feeling guilty you run in thought towards tomorrow's light.

We do not deserve that second chance, nor do we ever earn—the wages of our blessings. On we go but never learn—On we go still grasping out for what we think we need. Greedy for the gains of life . . . Ears deaf when others plead—For what you could supply . . . Night comes once more. Pay what you owe—Try again—then into tomorrow you can safely go.

The Benefit Of The Doubt

What does it matter after all what someone did or said?—Looking back it seems quite small when big things lie ahead—The unkind word should never ever be allowed to wreak—havoc in the home or heart, so think before you speak.

Does it really matter who was right or who was wrong—so long as relationships remain unbroken, just as strong—Never let a grievance fester. Draw the poison out—Give both enemy and friend the benefit of the doubt.

Somehow, Joy Comes Back

You thought you would never recover from the pain of a broken heart—when life's crystal bowl had been shattered—and the pieces flung apart.

But love has a sure way of dealing with human loss and lack . . . For time brings its own gentle healing—and somehow—Joy comes back.

The Rising Sun

Light precedes the rising sun that spreads a fiery fan—at the windows looking east where rays of glory span—the brightening horizon where the clouds gold-tipped make way—to prepare a royal welcome for the coming day.

We, too, should greet the sun's return as we would greet a king—for we know not what to us this new born day will bring . . . Blessed are we to stand and see the splendour of its birth—bringing life and light unto the edges of the earth.

A New Face In The Looking-Glass

Money, time and trouble you expend upon the care—of yourself; the part you see, the skin, the hands, the hair . . . But what about the inner self, the part that's not on view—the brain, the mind, the heart—the other part, the other you.

If you spent more time in training thoughts to go the way—of kindness and unselfishness, your own small part to play—to make the world a better place—you'd soon begin to see—a new face in the looking glass, the you that you could be.

Christmas

*O*nce again a song of joy resounds around the earth—the song that tells the wondrous story of the holy birth—of Him who made the worlds, the stars and every living thing. He, Redeemer and Messiah: Israel's promised King.

Christians, sing and sing again the song of Christmas Day—Tell the message of the angels and to all men say—Glory to God in the Highest, for the Christ is come to us—to proclaim a truth so simple, yet so marvellous.

Put the tawdry toys away. Let now your voice be heard—in praise of Him who was Himself the incarnated Word.

Time To Make Time

You make the time for making the pleasures you pursue—You make the time for taking the time it takes to do—the things that feed the ego and bolster up your pride—when the tiny whisper of conscience is denied.

But what time is devoted to inner questioning?—How many minutes do you spend on planning how to bring—something good to somebody struggling on their way—lightening the burden of someone's busy day?

Crossing Your Bridges

*N*ever cross your bridges till the bridge comes into view. Never go to meet your problems. Wait a day or two—Circumstances change that rearrange the sorted pack. Never take a load before it's placed upon your back.

Half life's many miseries upon ourselves we bring—Yet how often comes along the unexpected thing . . . Trust not in yourself, clever tricks and common sense. Look beyond yourself and trust the ways of Providence.

Save!

*I*n these spendthrift extravagant days—We grope through a dark and crowded maze—Where moral values are cast aside—foundations crumble and subside . . . In former times we were told to save—what the hand of Providence gave. Spend is the order of today. But our fathers used to say—Save. Conserve. Redeem the past. To honest principles holding fast.

Let us resolve if given time—To purify this pit of crime. Rebuilding our once-loved land anew—on what is righteous, good and true—Saving the wreckage of the years—Saving with our toil and tears . . . Save the hedge, the tree, the lane—from vandal's hand and acid rain . . . save our souls and pray that we—discover our lost identity.

Little Parcels

*T*here's so much trouble in the world you often wonder why—some folks like to keep it brewing just to satisfy—selfish aims and petty minds, establishing the right—to keep the trouble on the boil, to argue and to fight.

Such a waste of precious time, when Time is on the move—and every moment brings a chance to learn and to improve—Self, self, self—how boring and how futile life must be—wrapped up in a little parcel labelled . . . All for me.

The Life-Saver

Can you bank on anything in these uncertain days?—Can you trust the word of him who deals in devious ways?—Dare you lean on promises that rest on quaking ground?—Would you place your faith in things unstable and unsound?

In this world of selfishness, of anarchy and crime—The wise reach for The Book that has withstood the test of time—The Book that spreads throughout the world the Law: God's golden rule—Life-line for the young, the old, the scholar and the fool.

Autumn

*T*he first faint hint of what is yet to be—a pinkish tint upon the cherry tree—The old Virginia creepers turning red around the timbers of the garden shed—Lovely in its dying, yet how beautiful.—September's golden leaves: the autumn miracle.

As sure as clocks and calendars—the year when growing old—cloaks the woods in glory—bronze, crimson, amber, gold—The fires of Nature's making, the flames no man can stay: the mighty conflagration that runs from day to day—Like torches blaze the branches in wood and garden bower—September fades but not before it lives its finest hour.

Let Life Begin Anew

*E*very day that's granted you let life begin again. Do not cling to memories that leave a stab of pain. Never hold on to a grudge that rankles in the heart. Every day a new adventure and another start.

Never ruin in advance your chances of success—by brooding thoughts of failure and unhappiness. Don't invite more trouble if you want to get along—by constantly remembering the things that went all wrong.

Make amends for past mistakes while there is time to try. Do not leave it till tomorrow lest the chance slip by . . . Let the dawn ring up the curtain on a lovely view. Every day get up and say that life begins anew.

Index

INDEX